What Is Creative Nonfiction?

Charlotte Guillain

heinemann raintree

To contact Capstone Global Library please call 800-747-4992, or visit our web site
www.capstonepub.com

Edited by Clare Lewis and Penny West
Designed by Philippa Jenkins and Tim Bond
Picture research by Gina Kammer
Originated by Capstone Global Library Ltd
Produced by Helen McCreath
Printed and bound by CTPS

19 18 17 16 15
10 9 8 7 6 5 4 3 2 1

Library of Congress Cataloging-in-Publication Data
Guillain, Charlotte.
  What is creative nonfiction? / Charlotte Guillain.
     pages cm.—(Connect with text)
  Includes bibliographical references and index.
  ISBN 978-1-4109-8034-2 (hb)—ISBN 978-1-4109-8041-0 (ebook) 1. Creative nonfiction—Juvenile literature. 2. Reportage literature—Juvenile literature. 3. Prose literature—Juvenile literature. 4. Authorship—Juvenile literature. I. Title.
  PN145.G7788 2015
     808.02—dc23   2014049787

Acknowledgments
The author and publisher are grateful to the following for permission to reproduce copyright material:
Alamy: © razorpix, 19; Capstone Studio: Karon Dubke, 7, 8, 16, 17, 20, 21, 22; Corbis: © Bettmann, 26; Getty Images: Agence France Presse, 6, Print Collector, 9; Landov: dpa/KATJA LENZ, 12; Library of Congress, 27; Newscom: EPA/JON HRUSA, 19, Jamie Grill Blend Images/JGI, 29, Photoshot/Starstock/Jonathon Short, 10, ZUMAPRESS/Henglein And Steets, 4; Shutterstock: Andresr, 15, Anneka, 5, ikeriderlondon, 28, Blend Images, 24, Catalin Petolea, 25, Robnroll, 13, Ryan Rodrick Beiler, 11

Every effort has been made to contact copyright holders of any material reproduced in this book. Any omissions will be rectified in subsequent printings if notice is given to the publisher.

Contents

Some words are shown in bold, **like this**. You can find
out what they mean by looking in the glossary.

A World of Nonfiction

We read for many different reasons. We read web sites and newspapers to find out what is going on in the world. We read stories, poems, and comics to discover new worlds and imaginary characters who can show us all kinds of adventures. There are two main types of text that we read: **fiction** and **nonfiction**.

We read nonfiction on posters and signs to help us find our way around.

Ask your friends to recommend something you wouldn't normally read and see if you like it.

Fiction is writing that has been completely made up by the writer. It has characters and a story from the writer's imagination. Nonfiction is not made up. It is about facts—real things that have happened. Nonfiction gives us the information we need as we go through our lives. Nonfiction can be articles in magazines or the instructions for a new computer game. The information books you find in your school library are nonfiction. This book is about **creative nonfiction**.

Text around you

Do you prefer reading fiction or nonfiction? Try reading a type of text that you would never normally pick up. You might be surprised how much you enjoy it!

What Is Creative Nonfiction?

Creative nonfiction is sometimes called literary nonfiction. It is the closest type of **nonfiction** to **fiction** because of the language and style of the writing. Unlike other types of nonfiction, creative nonfiction tries to affect the reader's senses and emotions. This means the writer might create a lot of descriptive text that uses **adjectives** and **adverbs**. He or she could also use language with features such as **similes**, **metaphors**, and **alliteration**. All of these make writing more colorful and appealing.

Martin Luther King, Jr., made a famous speech in 1963 calling for peace and equality for all Americans. In his speech, he used many metaphors, such as "the solid rock of brotherhood" and "the valley of despair."

Creative nonfiction is usually written in the **past tense** and the **third person**. **Autobiographies** and personal accounts are written in the **first person**, since the writer is describing his or her own life.

Text tips!

If you're writing a piece of creative nonfiction text, think about how you can make your writing more colorful. You don't just want to write the bare facts. Instead, you should appeal to your reader's senses and include some exciting description.

What Types of Creative Nonfiction Are There?

Examples of **creative nonfiction** include:

- speeches
- **biographies** about famous people's lives
- **autobiographies** about the author's own life
- travel writing about the author's experiences in different parts of the world
- essays on a range of subjects
- **eyewitness accounts** of important events
- articles in magazines and newspapers.

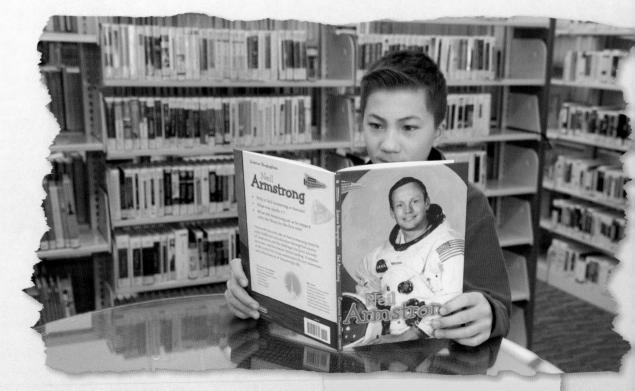

A biography is a piece of writing about a person's life and work.

These types of text are found in printed books and in digital formats. People usually read creative nonfiction **chronologically**. This means that they start reading at the beginning and work through the book to the end. It wouldn't normally make sense to jump right into the middle of the book and start reading.

Creative nonfiction contains accurate information and lots of details about the people, place, and time being described. The writer writes in a way that will hook readers in so they want to keep reading to the end.

Text in history

Some of the most famous books ever written are creative nonfiction. Charles Darwin's book about the natural world, *On the Origin of Species*, was published in 1859. Many scientists have presented new ideas in creative nonfiction throughout history.

Who Writes Creative Nonfiction?

People who write **creative nonfiction** know a lot about their subject. Often they are writing about personal experiences—for example, their life and work, in an **autobiography**. They may write about a journey they took in a piece of travel writing. Other writers of creative nonfiction are specialists in a subject they've studied. They might be scientists or other experts. They have done a lot of research and want to share what they've learned with a wider audience.

Lots of people enjoy reading travel writing because they can learn about different parts of the world without traveling anywhere!

Other creative nonfiction is written by
journalists. They write articles and essays about
important events or people. Some people write
creative nonfiction online, on blogs or web sites.
Speeches are written for important people to give
at special events. The best speeches are often
written down for people to read afterward, and
this is another type of creative nonfiction.

Text tips!

If you're going to write a piece of creative
nonfiction, choose your subject carefully. It
needs to be something you know a lot about,
unless you have lots of time to research
something new!

Why Do People Read Creative Nonfiction?

Many people enjoy reading **creative nonfiction**. If you're interested in a particular subject, it can be fascinating to read what an expert has written about it. Lots of readers like to read **biographies** of famous people to learn more about their lives. Some people like to read travel writing before they visit a new place. This helps them to learn more about the history of the country and the people who live there.

People like reading creative nonfiction because they enjoy the style and language that the writer uses. Many readers like the way creative nonfiction gives them information, but is written in a way that is similar to **fiction**. Today, many people get a lot of information from the Internet. They like to read creative nonfiction, such as articles and **eyewitness accounts**, online.

Text in history

If you're interested in history, you might enjoy *A Little History of the World* by Ernst Gombrich. He wrote this book in 1935, taking the reader through human history from the Stone Age onward.

Lots of creative
nonfiction is
available on
the Internet.

What Are the Features of Creative Nonfiction?

Creative nonfiction can include the following features:

- This type of **nonfiction** often looks very similar to **fiction**. Creative nonfiction can be divided up into chapters, and the writer will often use language similar to that used in fiction.

- The reader is usually supposed to read a piece of creative nonfiction from start to finish. Reading creative nonfiction is like reading a story. It has a clear beginning and end, and there are exciting and dramatic moments.

- The writing in a piece of creative nonfiction will move toward a clear ending.

- This sort of nonfiction text might have **appendices** that give extra information at the back of the book. There might be an **index**, too.

- Like many other types of nonfiction, creative nonfiction tends to use a lot of transitional time words, such as "first," "next," "meanwhile," and "afterward."

Text around you

Look in your school or local library for a **biography** of a person who interests you. Can you spot any typical features of creative nonfiction? Is the book divided into chapters like a **novel**?

Reading about a famous person's life can be fascinating.

Autobiography

An **autobiography** is a piece of **creative nonfiction** that the author writes about his or her own life and achievements. Famous people often write autobiographies because many people are interested in their lives and how they became well known.

The South African leader Nelson Mandela wrote about his life in his autobiography, *Conversations with Myself.*

Autobiographies can have the following features:

- The text is broken up into sections or chapters.
- The writer takes the reader through the stages of his or her life, usually in **chronological** order.
- They often include personal details and memories.
- They might include photos of different parts of the writer's life.
- Autobiographies are likely to focus on the part of the writer's life that he or she is best known for.

Text in history

Roald Dahl (1916–1990) wrote two autobiographies. The first, *Boy: Tales of Childhood*, is about his early life and time in school. *Going Solo* is about his life as a grown-up before he became a writer, including his experiences as a pilot in World War II (1939–1945).

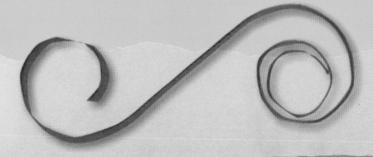

How to Write Creative Nonfiction: Starting an Autobiography

Many **autobiographies** start with the writer's first memory. Why not write about your earliest memory to share with your friends and family?

1. Think about your childhood and look at photos of when you were little. What early memories can you remember?

2. Choose one memory and write notes about it. Do you have all the information about the event, such as the date, the place, and your age at the time?

3. Start to write your memory in a first **draft**. Write in the **first person** and **past tense**. Try to describe the events in the order that they happened.

4. Go through your first draft. Make your writing more interesting with **adjectives** or **adverbs**. Use **similes** or **metaphors** to help the reader to picture what you are describing. Tell the reader how you were feeling at the time.

5. Can you add any useful transitional time words, such as "next," "afterward," or "meanwhile"? This helps to make the sequence of events clearer.

6. Check your spelling and grammar!

7. Write or type a final version of your memory and share it with a friend or family member. Add photos if you like.

Biography and Historical Writing

A **biography** is also about a person's life or part of his or her life. However, it is written by someone else—a biographer. The biographer has to research the person's life, either by interviewing the person or people who knew the person. The biographer also studies letters, diaries, and other information.

People who write about historical events have to do similar research to biographers. They spend a lot of time finding accurate information. They try not to be influenced by other writers' opinions about events.

How many biographies have you read?

Text around you

Ask your librarian if he or she can recommend any biographies about someone you're interested in. Or you could look for biographies of people involved in something that interests you, such as sports or science. Does reading about the person help you to understand his or her achievements?

Biographies and historical writing often have the following features:

- Presentation of the events in **chronological** order, as they happened.
- Quotations from letters, diaries, and other written sources.
- The writer's own opinions or judgments about the subject and why things happened the way they did.
- Photos, maps, and other illustrations.

How to Write Creative Nonfiction:
Retelling an Event in History

Write about an historical event that happened in your local area.

1. Talk to a relative or a teacher to help you choose an event. Think of some questions about what happened. Write the questions down and leave space for the answers.

2. It's time to research the answers! Check library books and the Internet. Only visit web sites that provide information you can trust, such as those of museums and important organizations. You could also visit a museum or other historical site.

3. Write down your findings in the space beneath each question.

4. Now plan how you are going to structure your writing. You'll need an **introduction** and a **conclusion**. Make sure you include details about dates, places, and people.

5. Use your notes to write your text in your own words. Make sure the facts you found in different places match up— otherwise, you'll need to do more research to get the right answers!

6. Check your spelling and grammar and make sure that you've written the text in the correct order.

7. Add photos or maps to make the text even more interesting.

8. Share your writing with your family, friends, or teacher.

Speeches

People write speeches for other people to hear. Many important speeches are written down for people to read afterward, too. Some speeches, such as Martin Luther King, Jr.'s, "I Have a Dream" speech, have become very famous.

Susan B. Anthony (1820–1906) used memorable speeches to help win the right to vote for women in the United States.

Text in history

Winston Churchill (1874–1965) led the United Kingdom during World War II (1939–1945). He made a famous speech during the war that used repetition:

"…we shall fight on the beaches, we shall fight on the landing grounds, we shall fight in the fields and in the streets, we shall fight in the hills…"

Many good speeches have some of the following features:

- Words or phrases are repeated so that they stick in the listener's or reader's mind. Martin Luther King, Jr., repeated "Let freedom ring…" in his speech.
- They sometimes include **rhetorical questions**. These questions don't expect an answer, but they make the listener think about what the speaker is saying.
- A speech often talks to the listener or reader directly. It tries to persuade him or her to agree with a certain point of view or to appeal to the person's feelings.
- Speeches may include **anecdotes**.
- There are often longer sentences followed by shorter sentences, which stand out.

How to Write Creative Nonfiction: Writing a Speech

Write a speech about something you really care about.

1. Pick a subject that really matters to you for your speech. For example, you could talk about why it is so important to care for pets properly.

2. Start by introducing yourself and your subject. Explain why this subject matters to you.

3. Break your speech up into different points. When you have written about each point, give examples to show why it matters. You could include personal stories about your own experience.

4. Can you repeat some words or phrases to get your listener's attention?

5. Include some **rhetorical questions**—these are questions you ask when you don't really expect an answer. They just make the listener think.

6. Include some short, snappy sentences after a few long ones. These add variety and make the speech sound more interesting.

7. Write a good **conclusion** to your speech. It should stick in readers' minds and persuade them that your ideas are right!

8. When you've finished writing your speech, practice reading it. When you are ready, read it out loud to your family and friends!

Glossary

adjective word that describes a noun

adverb word that describes a verb

alliteration when words start with the same first letter

anecdote personal story

appendix (plural: appendices) extra information at the end of a book

autobiography story of the writer's life

biography story of someone else's life

chronological in the order that things happened

conclusion ending to a piece of writing

creative nonfiction writing that uses literary techniques usually used in fiction to report on real-life events

draft early attempt at a piece of writing

eyewitness account story of real events told by someone who was there

fiction story that is not true

first person when a writer uses "I" and "me"

index list of words in a book with page numbers where you will find that word

introduction beginning of a piece of writing that explains what the writing will be about

metaphor when something is described as being another thing

nonfiction writing about real-life facts

novel long story

past tense writing that describes events that have already happened

rhetorical question question asked to have an impact on the reader or listener; it doesn't normally expect an answer

simile when one thing is compared to another

third person when a writer talks about "her," "him," or "they"

Find Out More

To learn more about creative nonfiction in all its forms, take a look at the following books. These include examples of biography, autobiography, and historical events. You could also use the web sites listed below to research a subject that interests you. Use your findings and the "How to" topics in this book to test out your new creative nonfiction writing skills!

Books

Edison, Erin. *Susan B. Anthony* (Great Women in History). N. Mankato, Minn.: Capstone, 2013.

Gombrich, Ernst. *A Little History of the World.* New Haven, Conn.: Yale University, 2005.

Hunter, Nick. *Charles Darwin* (Science Biographies). Chicago: Raintree, 2014.

Jazynka, Kitson. *Martin Luther King, Jr.* (National Geographic Readers: Bios). Washington, D.C.: National Geographic, 2012.

Mandela, Nelson, abridged by Chris van Wyk. *Long Walk to Freedom.* New York: Little, Brown, 2014.

Web sites

Facthound offers a safe, fun way to find Internet sites related to this book. All of the sites on Facthound have been researched by our staff.

Here's all you do:
Visit www.facthound.com
Type in this code: 9781410980342

Index